UNIFORM CIVIL CODE
ONE NATION ONE LAW

First Edition

2017

WRITTEN BY
Akash Kamal Mishra

Published by :

    Createspace –An Amazon Company
    www.createspace.com

Edited by :

    Dr. Pooja Roydas Gupta
    Ph.D.,M.B.A. (HR, Finance), M.A. (Economics)

    &
    Ms. Mahima Sharma
    Purs. B.A.LL.B. (Hons.)

Cover by :

    Amazon.com, Inc

First Edition : 2017

Price : **$ 6**

©

All rights including copyrights is reserved with author.

ISBN : **978-19756-68723**

Printed & Sold by :
CreateSpace, a DBA of On-Demand Publishing, LLC

DISCLAMER

Uniform Civil Code : One Nation One Law is a book made for sharing the concept of New Developments and Changing Agenda of the UCC.

This publication is made on the condition and understanding that the content and the information it contains are merely for society awareness as a reference and must not be taken as having the authority of being binding in anyways on Publisher & Author.

Printer, Publisher & Author are not responsible for any kind of damages or loss caused to any person on accounts of error / omission in advertently crept in.

No one neither Author, Publisher, nor Printer is liable for any breach of copyright...

Happy Reading!!!!!!!!!!!!!!!

DEDICATED TO

Late Shri Badri Prasad Mishra
{My Elder Grand Father}

About Author

Akash Kamal Mishra S./of Dr. Shri Kamal Mishra born on 22 June at Rewa , Madhya Pradesh, India which is famous for the origin of **WHITE TIGER** in a very small village with a distance of 150km from birth place named **Sabicha Post. Sihawal District – Sidhi , Madhya Pradesh, India.**

He has completed his entire schooling with Physics, Chemistry, Biology from Morition Public Senior Secondary School, Sidhi Madhya Pradesh.

He Became an author during his graduation time at the age of 21 and published his 1st book on **An Overview On Cyber Crime & Security , Volume-I with ISBN : 978-15-45344-62-0** now available in online stores of Amazon's and latter published 2nd book on **Digital Signature – The Need of Cashless Society with ISBN : 978-15-46382-53-9** .

Being an author he has been awarded by many world famous luminaries and has been recognized as the **cyber expert** in very short age. Also he has been awarded **Young writer 2016, District Icon Award 2016** ,by the **cyber security expert of India**, **Inspector General of Police Indore**, and also the prestigious **Digital India Award - Silver Medal from Ministry of Information Technology Government of India .**

Currently he is Pursuing B.A.LL.B.(Hons.) from Indore Institute of Law Indore, India which is Affiliated to Devi Ahilya University and Bar Council of India.

He has completed his diploma in Certified Information Security Engineer, Certified Ethical Hacker from EC-Council.

He has been registered as the **DISTINGUISHED MEMBER - INTERNATIONAL COUNCIL OF JURISTS, LONDON, UNITED KINGDOM.**

Akash Kamal Mishra started working for seminars on cyber safety and had taken 32 Seminars on Cyber Safety with in association of Indore Administrative Department, Indore and had interacted with 6000+ Students of various cities .

~~~~~

FROM THE DESK OF AUTHOR

I would like to give my sincere sense of gratitude to my parents and siblings who has supported me for this work the Uniform Civil Code : One Nation One Law.

I present here the recent developments in India law relating to the much-debated Uniform Civil Code it's concept of New Developments and Changes made in it's Agenda .

Hope that this book will definitely prove beneficial to everyone to understand the meaning and the concept of Uniform Civil Code.

Akash Kamal Mishra
Pursuing B.A.LL.B(HONS.)

FOREWORD

Expert practice has changed dramatically over the last 10 years, and as if mirroring the digital world, albeit at a slower pace, it continues to change.

To mark the footsteps of the nation and emerging lawyers at large, this book brings to light a very important, yet novice topic, 'one nation, one law'. The text provides a comprehensive update of the relevant law and procedure, with a clear exposition of the many changes in the judicial system over the last few years, familiarity and indulgence of which is essential to opinion evidence that meets legal requirements and fulfils its proper function in the litigation process.

The book unveils the prominence of India's vast legislature and also speaks of the various challenges that had to be gone through while bringing this to practice.

Through this book the young but matured author Mr. Akash Kamal Mishra identifies the need to educate the society about legal pluralism and also about the major leap the Civil legislature of the nation is taking to passage all laws from static to dynamic.

I am sure that readers will find this edition an invaluable aid to legal understanding and to the enhancement of their skill set.

It is accessible, interesting and informative, and will serve further to improve the quality of the study of legal uniformity.

This timely book is an important intellectual service for research scholars, judges, lawyers, law teachers & students.

My heartiest congratulations to Mr. Akash Kamal Mishra for bringing this book.

A. C. Agg

Dr. Adish C. Aggarwala
President
**International Council of Jurists,
London, United Kingdom**

INDEX

UNIFORM CIVIL CODE – ONE NATION ONE LAW

1. Introduction..01-08
2. The Problem of managing difference & legal pluralism..09-11
3. The challenge of legal pluralism for independent India...12-18
4. The Relevance of history...........................19-26
5. Hindu law & religion as India's dominant system in plural context...27-32
6. Learning to respect differences in independent India...33-38
7. The persistence of legal differences in modern India...39-45
8. Contribution of the legislature in interaction with court..46-53
9. Towards legal uniformity despite personal laws....54-59
10. Supporting evidence from growing uniformity of Indian divorce laws...................................60-63
11. Conclusion...64-74

REFERENCES..75-88

I
Introduction

Postcolonial India's modernist ambition to have a Uniform Civil Code, impressively written into Article 44 of the Indian Constitution of 1950 as a non-justiciable Directive Principle of State Policy, concerns not just an Indian problem but a universal predicament for lawyers and legal systems. What is the relationship between personal status laws and general state-made laws? To what extent should the formal law allow for, or seek to restrain, the legal implications of religious and socio-cultural diversity? To what extent does a state, whether secular or not, actually have power and legitimacy to decree and enforce legal uniformity? There are many more agendas at play here than simply the central issue of legal authority, focused on the power of the law, or simply "religion" v. "law", or "culture" v. "law", as we are often still led to believe.

I present here the recent developments in India's law relating to the much-debated Uniform Civil Code agenda to illustrate that Indian law today increasingly turns its back on supposedly European or "Western" models, and has been developing its own country-specific and situation-sensitive methods of handling complex socio-legal issues. This may contain some important lessons for European lawyers, specifically in terms of managing cultural diversity through plurality-conscious legal intervention, rather than the traditional insistence on state-centric legal uniformity.

The key lesson from this evidence is that personal status laws may well endure and survive the much-desired uniformity of legal reforms all over Asia and Africa, and probably elsewhere, too. The future of the world lies evidently not in simplistic legal uniformity, but in considered, carefully weighed respect for diversity. Globalisation, we are told elsewhere, comes out prominently as localisation,[1] creating new hybrid entities of ever-growing plurality. Therefore, we must learn to handle and understand more deeply how plural legal arrangements operate and what their potential is for making progressive improvements to human lives and sustainable development.

At first, India's persuasively official postcolonial programme for introduction of a Uniform Civil Code seemed to follow the West, embodying a newly invigorated civilising mission, a clarion call for consolidated nation-building and the achievement of legal modernity through top-down state-driven secularising reforms. This exciting national vision for development was embraced with fervent enthusiasm by Eurocentric and Europhilic modernists everywhere in the world and India received much praise for this agenda item. Many Indians, including some Supreme Court judges, fired this supposedly "progressive" ambition with authoritative and seemingly persuasive calls for fundamental reforms, demanding less confusion in the jungle of personal laws, sometimes even claiming to be able to rid India of "culture" and "tradition", "customs" and "religion", all those contaminating and supposedly "extra-legal" elements that allegedly impede proper functioning of a state-led legal framework.

But roughly half a century later, soon after the turn of the millennium, India's socio-legal reality has evidently taken a different trajectory than modernists expected. The jungle of legal plurality is still there. We find more state law, but no Uniform Civil Code. The perennial calls for legal uniformity have become quieter and certainly much less convincing if one considers the new, incompletely studied developments that have occurred in the meantime.

These illustrate the hybrid nature of all law and thus teach us about the central relevance and urgent necessity of understanding legal pluralism as a living reality. By 2001, and not accidentally – as we shall see - two weeks after 9/11, it became clearer that post-colonial India did not in fact aim for the kind of Uniform Civil Code that so many modernist observers and stakeholders had been vigorously demanding. Instead, as I have shown elsewhere,[2].

India re-learnt an ancient lesson about demanding the impossible, culturally envisaged as asking for the moon. In the ancient Indian story, the child god Krishna asks his mother Yashoda to give him the moon as a toy and the clever doting mother hands him a mirror with a reflection of the moon.

In post-modern India, quick-footed thinking of this kind has now resulted in well-considered production of a mirror image of the desired object of the Uniform Civil Code in the form of a harmonised personal law system. A motherly central state and its core institutions, an activist and very powerful Supreme Court and a Parliament not incapable of speedy action, deliberately put here in that order, have taken well-choreographed steps to achieve this particular outcome.

India, as I shall show, has quite consciously over decades – and thus not by accident - developed a fascinating reflection of the original ideal of the Uniform Civil Code, in the form of a sophisticated, harmonised system of legal regulation that maintains and skillfully uses the input of personal status laws and yet achieves a measure of legal uniformity. While the boundaries of Indian general law and personal laws have thus become ever more fuzzy, neither Hindu law nor Muslim law, nor indeed any of the various other, partly seriously outdated minority personal laws, have been abolished by these new legal developments.

The legal jungle, as indicated, has become thicker. And yet, contrary to what secular modernists allege and fear, this development is extremely progressive, apart from being quite instructive for global legal theory.

In India, a new civil code was earlier, quite simplistically deemed to be able to pick the best elements from various legal systems.[3] This convenient mix-and-match image reflects a blind belief in legal positivism which borders on dictatorial illusions and feeds of course on oversimplified Austinian and Napoleonic images of law-making. Instead, Indian family laws have been skillfully reformed and harmonised in such a way that the newly configured Indian legal system of the post 9/11 era has extremely sensitively built the various traditional legal systems and new social welfare concerns into a gradually consolidated form of post-modern social welfare law.

The conceptual roots of this evidently go back to ancient Indic concepts of macrocosmic and microcosmic duty, and thus to indigenous natural laws and related socio-legal concepts. More tangible legal foundations of this plurality-conscious legal regime have been developing almost imperceptibly through positivist legal interventions, at least since the mid-1970s under Indira Gandhi's much-debated Emergency rule. Notably, these foundations have emerged more clearly in September 2001, but since then they have been embellished by new statutes and case law almost year by year.

Since 2001, the contours of India's new welfare-conscious legal structures have become particularly clearly manifested in India's radical post-1985 regime of post-marital maintenance entitlement for all ex-wives until death or remarriage, building on the world-famous Shah Bano case of 1985.[4] This was followed by the Hindu Succession (Amendment) Act of 2005, the Prohibition of Child Marriage Act of 2006 and most recently the remarkable Maintenance and Welfare of Parents and Senior Citizens Act of 2007. Taken together, these purposeful innovations constitute to a large extent deliberately silent dramatic readjustment of social welfare laws in India, which may be an economically booming country today, but also remains a place teeming with hundreds of millions of people living below the poverty line.

There are powerful constitutional agendas here requiring the Indian state to intervene in gendered imbalances and to construct a more effective social welfare net that does not require monetary input from the state, but relies on social and moral normative orders to provide remedies.

The present article concentrates on highlighting these interconnected new developments and crucial changes of agenda in the Indian legal system, which still displays and operates an intricate combination of general laws and personal laws. These recent ultra-modern (probably rather, post-modern) developments have not been openly debated, it seems, because too many stakeholders and academics oppose, mostly for ideological reasons, what has been happening on the ground. The resulting deliberate silence has the consequence that knowledge and scholarship on Indian laws continue to be seriously misled and misguided about crucial aspects of the deeply contested nature of current Indian legal developments.

Much is becoming certain, however: India does not, and simply cannot, follow the West's positivism-centered legal trajectory, because it could not survive as a viable nation if its legal system ignored persistent internal diversities and the socio-legal predicaments of hundreds of millions of disadvantaged people. Indian law, maybe even more so than in the past, must remain diversity-conscious today. It has to carefully manage this diversity in ways that many observers find not only incredibly complex, but plainly incredible. However, the slow train of Indian democracy moves on through history, while neighbouring Pakistan, Sri Lanka and Bangladesh have faced repeated derailments caused by lack of democratic management skills and deficient respect for plurality. Still, the outcome for India is not "the moon" of a Uniform Civil Code, but rather, an amazingly close mirror image of this ideal that seems to work in practice.

Thus, going here beyond the partly ideological struggles that obstruct our views of current Indian legal developments, I seek to argue that these recent Indian legal innovations contain important lessons for the world as a whole on how to manage cultural diversity through legal interventions.

In brief, my central argument is that post 9/11 India acts like a management guru to the globalising world about how to handle cultural diversity through a sophisticated system of legal pluralism, relying on concepts and experiences of the past, but also looking to the future, not afraid to experiment with new, potentially explosive mixes of ingredients in the legal laboratory.

*****

II
The "Problem" of Managing Difference and Legal Pluralism

Today, no country in the world only has one type of people within its borders, since migration is not only an ancient human phenomenon, but has become ever more ubiquitous.[5] A much underrated legal consequence of this has been that personal status laws everywhere actually continue to migrate with people and then impact the application of family laws, making them ever more international.[6] In socio-legal reality, such personal status laws of recent migrants, becoming what I have recently called "ethnic implants" rather than formal transplants,[7] raise important new questions, especially in the global North, about how we should manage cultural diversity in law.[8] Questions about the extent of recognition of such "new" forms of legal diversity are arising more frequently. Such uncomfortable questions may still be brushed aside by formally trained lawyers in many jurisdictions by insistence on legal dogma, national cohesion and a predilection for legal uniformity. All of these factors are conceptually and emotionally reinforced where a country's legal history suggests a clear-cut trajectory of movement from earlier customary laws and local diffuseness towards national uniformity, as embodied in the common law tradition of England, or the legal histories of many continental European countries. But all over Asia and Africa, in Latin America and elsewhere, historically grown personal status laws have not simply gone away because states wish them to vanish. Different legal histories co-exist and continue to operate, often unofficially.

This is increasingly recognised in these regions and in global jurisprudence as valuable, giving rise to post-modern reconfigurations of what commonsensical sustainable laws should take account of.[9] Foreign transplants may be officially powerful,[10] but may not reach every village and certainly not every citizen's heart or mind. Often banished to the realm of unofficial laws,[11] innumerable personal status laws survive particularly strongly in the global South, continue to prosper below the formal legal surface, and often form part of the second type of what Chiba calls "official law".[12] Since all countries appear to have their own culture-specific legal histories and have constructed their legal systems over time as best suited to their people or leaders, there is not one "law of the world", no one model that every state could just follow. A lot of work remains to be done by scholars to understand this fully, and lawyers are often not at the forefront of thinking in this field.[13] Legal minds have often been numbed, it seems, by positivist temptations of asking for the moon, even decreeing that the moon should appear.

This means that legal pluralism, in a globally interconnected world which has not developed one world law despite many strenuous efforts, has become ever more important as a legal topic. Globalisation has actually increased the local and regional diversity of religions, customs and laws, and thus impacts almost everywhere directly on formal legal structures. While the desire for equality-conscious and nationally uniform legal regulation is of course strong and justice, we are still often told, means equality rather than equity, the reality remains that legal pluralism is a fact and remains the norm.[14]

*****

III
The Challenge Of Legal Pluralism For Independent India

Explicit recognition of the reality of legal pluralism, of course, questions and challenges long-dominant, clearly Eurocentric, positivist presumptions about the desirability of legal uniformity and its link with "rule of law". As a former colonial territory, India has not been immune from such influences and presumptions, but actually has a richly documented ancient experience of operating in complex systems of legal pluralism,[15] which centuries of Muslim rule and British colonial domination could not erase. The postcolonial Indian state, divorced from Islamic Pakistan, was partly tempted to follow Western-dominated legal and political thinking, but was also pulled by M.K. Gandhi towards ancient Hindu concepts of governance and law. Fortunately, the leaders at the time sensed that India as a composite whole would have to make sense of its own plurality-conscious heritage in the light of new socio-legal realities and would quite clearly have to live with legal pluralism, even if this was not always going to be easy.

One may observe today that this often tortuous experience has actually turned out to be for the benefit of the country as a growing nation and also that it contrasts favourably with India's neighbours.

When British India was carved up at midnight on 14/15 August 1947 between India and Pakistan, Pakistan fooled itself into believing that it could become a country for Muslims, with disastrous results, as we know today, even for Muslim minorities, let alone others. India, however, was evidently aware that post-colonial Bharat, the sovereign Republic of India, would need to be the home to many different kinds of people with many different kinds of laws.

So after ferocious debates in the Constituent Assembly, the Indians eventually inserted into their Constitution of 1950 a compromise programme for the future, which seemed to privilege legal uniformity and raised an expectation that there should eventually be a Uniform Civil Code. This overarching policy aim, as an ambition for the future, was laid down in Article 44 of the Indian Constitution of 1950, a Directive Principle of State Policy.

I show here that the original aim and ambition of a Uniform Civil Code for all Indians as a common code shared by all citizens, as originally envisaged by the Constitution makers, has simply not materialised – today we have a mirror image of that envisaged legal uniformity. I also predict that complete legal uniformity will never materialise in India or anywhere in the world. Indeed we see, almost 60 years after the first postcolonial agenda for legal uniformity were set, how Indian family law has made skilful use of a different model of uniformity of laws, harmonisation, which the original law makers perhaps did not perceive as a viable option but which has turned out to be the dominant and official legal reality in India today.

This Indian method of operating a uniform law without having a codified Uniform Civil Code has gradually developed under our very noses over several decades. But most Indians, and also most academic observers, have not noticed this and the Indian state has had its own agenda for not telling people clearly what it was doing. Still, these are not accidental haphazard developments. The Indian state has apparently acted purposefully, albeit silently and surreptitiously, cautiously and gradually harmonising the various Indian personal laws along similar lines without challenging their status as separate personal laws. The Indian experience shows that this development does not require the admittedly dangerous radical step of a newly implemented uniform enactment in family law for all citizens.[16] Rather, India has devised a strategy of carefully planned minor changes over a long span of time, actually an intricate interplay between judicial activism and parliamentary intervention,[17] which has left the various bodies of personal law as separate entities. Post-modern India, therefore, seems to have found a rather exciting solution to the conundrum of legal uniformity which may well be a suitable model for many other countries.

As a result of this carefully planned strategy, the various Indian personal laws now look more like each other than ever, but they are still identifiable in terms of "ethnic" and "religious" identity as Hindu, Muslim, Parsi, and Christian law, not only by their titles, but also in substance. I suggest that this observation also holds true for Muslim law in India, despite its largely un-codified format, and the apparent reluctance of Muslim leaders and spokespersons to contemplate statutory legal reform. The fact that Indian Muslim law was not subjected to codification (as many Hindu nationalists have continued to demand) which pleased and reassured the Muslims, but it did not save Indian Muslim personal law from being affected by the post-modern reconstruction process. Rather incautiously, in fact, Indian Muslims themselves demanded a separate personal law after the Shah Bano decision.[18] We know today that they speedily got from Rajiv Gandhi's government what they wanted, namely a separate Muslim law enactment that appeared to exempt Muslims from the general law regulations of the Criminal Procedure Code, 1973.[19] But the substance of that law, as we should have understood from many High Court cases since at least 1988,[20] was not really different in material respects from the secular provisions of the 1973 Code which Muslims wanted to evade.

Essentially, Indian Muslims fell out of the frying pan into the fire by demanding a new separate law: Under section 3(1)(a) of the 1986 Act, a divorcing Muslim husband now became liable to potentially much higher maintenance payments to his ex-wife than under section 125 of the Criminal Procedure Code with its then upper limit of 500 Rupees, which is barely a few British pounds, or a few more euros, per month. The full extent of this clever legal engineering was buried rather than openly admitted in the many words of the Indian Supreme Court in the notable *Danial Latifi* case of 2001.[21] This decision was promulgated after 15 years of sitting on this initially hotly-debated constitutional petition, until September 2001, thus at a strategic moment, just two weeks after 9/11. The Court held that the *Shah Bano* case had been good law, thus reinforcing the general social welfare principle that Indian ex-husbands have to maintain their ex-wives until they die or remarry. Further, it was held that it remained perfectly legitimate for Indian law to make reasonable classifications between citizens by promulgating a separate Act for Muslims only. Thirdly - and this could have caused Muslim riots, but did not do so two weeks after 9/11 - it was firmly held that Indian Muslim husbands remained under an obligation to maintain their ex-wives, as laid down in section 3 of the 1986 Act,[22] already explained and held by many High Court decisions by that time.[23] Careful reading of these cases, thus, teaches that the Indian Constitution with its wider social welfare agenda would not, and could not, tolerate principled total exemption from social welfare agenda when matters of Muslim personal law were at stake. Thus, outwardly, it only *appears* as though Muslim personal law in India has remained largely uncodified *shari'a* law. In reality, it has been just as much subject to the skilful combined efforts of India's judiciary and Parliament to harmonise all Indian personal laws without abolishing the personal law system. So the Indian state tiptoed slowly and carefully around the issue of legal reforms, cleverly manipulative like an ancient Indian ruler inspired by the traditional Indian science of governance (*artha!"stra*). Ancient lessons about outwitting one's adversaries, here a potential inner enemy, had to be most skilfully employed. Indian Muslim law could not be allowed to remain outside the constitutional umbrella, but it also could not be abolished. So it actually helped the post-modern Indian state that Muslims, in an incautious moment, had demanded a separate statutory law for themselves. They promptly got it - but not on their terms, as we now know.

Hence Indian law has certainly not been static over the last 50-60 years. But the various subtle movements – often highly politicised and perceived as dangerous for communal harmony in a pluralistic state dominated by Hindus and Hindu concepts, have had several deeper silent agendas which have not been abandoned despite many communal riots, multiple accusations of fundamentalism and now terrorism. Led by the almost invisible hand of senior "secular" bureaucrats, India has by now virtually reached its aim of constructing a uniform personal law for all Indians through engineering much greater harmonisation of personal laws and thus achieving equality of all citizens in terms of substance. Admittedly, this is difficult to understand, and it seems hard to swallow for communal politicians and modernist scholars.

The continuing challenges of legal pluralism in a nation marked by unity in diversity, combined with the historically grounded resilience of the personal law system in India, thus mean that most Indians today, common citizens and academics alike, as well as most foreign observers, look with some puzzlement at a mirror image of the originally anticipated phenomenon of India's Uniform Civil Code. Indians, it seems then, are still almost as confused as Western legocentric scholars about the practical applications of plurality-conscious navigation. But somehow, post-modern India managed to navigate this. The next section seeks to explore briefly to what extent such acute plurality-consciousness may be rooted in Indian history.

IV
The Relevance of History

Post-colonial India entered what its first Prime Minister, Jawaharlal Nehru, called a "tryst with history" at the point of independence at midnight on 14/15 August 1947. A major task for the new government was setting the agenda for much-needed change to achieve a better future. But embarking on a new future is one thing, achieving development another; past and future need to be combined, as lawyers focusing on developmental issues have had to acknowledge again and again. History, thus, contains fruitful lessons as well as fetters on ambitions for radical legal reform.

Evolution rather than revolution was clearly the envisaged path of postcolonial Indian legal development and India could not simply abolish the personal law system overnight. Hence, as part of an intricate compromise, Article 44 in the Indian Constitution, as a Directive Principle of State Policy, laid down the original policy aim of secular postcolonial nation building. It aimed to achieve, gradually, rather than at once, more far-reaching equality for all citizens. Justice was not served on a silver platter, but began to move more within reach of the common citizen.[24] The somewhat pompously guaranteed right to equality in Article 14 of the Indian Constitution became a new *Grundnorm*, but was not thereby automatically turned into socio-legal reality.

Within the Fundamental Rights of the same Constitution, the qualified equality under Article 14 was matched with further important basic equality guarantees under Articles 15 and 16, which notably permit the Indian state to make several special protective provisions for certain classes of people, particularly women, children and members of historically disadvantaged communities. All of this reflects deep awareness that new laws do not create facts overnight and that the ideal of equality remained at best a long-term goal, certainly not socio-legal reality implemented by the stroke of a pen. Awareness of the limits of law, underpinning the new legal structures, also meant that various forms of protective discrimination would probably need to remain part of Indian law for a long time to come, however much fought over. For India, all these are lessons well learnt from history.

However, other ambitious Indian agenda for law reform were partly built on the legocentric claim that legal reform can happen fast, predominantly through secular codification; thus the law maker's pen would offer potent remedies in India today. The vision of this legislative ambition has remained powerful in many Indian minds. Tempted to be legal positivists at heart, with ambitions to reach modernity by jumping in leaps and bounds, many of India's citizens supported reformist agenda and expect further reforms. But exaggerated optimism was cooled down rather soon by Nehru's realisation that in order for law reform to be effective in society, people themselves would have to change their ways of doing things.[25]

Earlier, India's colonial rulers, after assumption of sovereignty in 1858, had engaged in massive law making by statute, creating Anglo-Indian law, a new official law composed of many statutes and cases. Similarly, postcolonial Indian law makers embarked on a phase of vigorous codification through statute and judicial precedent as part of the process of nation building. This led almost in a straight line directly to the rapid and dramatic failure of the Hindu Code Bill project of the early 1950s.[26]

By the 1980s, though, emerging post-modern legal scholars began to identify this propensity towards codification critically as dominant Western "model jurisprudence".[27] By then, Western-style positivism had managed to portray itself as advanced, modern, and thus superior. It occupies still today the moral high ground, albeit not without increasingly severe criticism.[28] But significantly, it was not part of earlier Indian legal history that law reforms occur predominantly through top-down legislation. India has other powerful memories of legal history, which has meant that it could and can creatively rely on different methods of setting agenda and implementing socially beneficial reforms.

But it seems that these historical lessons had gradually been overshadowed by colonial intervention. The idea that a developed legal system should appear in codified form was firmly implanted in the minds of scholars and lawyers, as well as historians and other social scientists, by the mid-nineteenth century. This kind of evolutionist thinking, traceable to Sir Henry Maine (see below), influenced not only the historical trajectory of English Common Law, but soon became a dominant global image, much criticised today.[29] Many people, not only lawyers, still think today of law automatically as a fixed set of rules made by the state in the form of codes. We are indeed, in our minds, tempted to essentialise law into a tool of codification, even a static body of codified rules. Even outside France or Continental Europe, the image of the Code Napoleon as an embodiment of law remains powerful,[30] also in the so-called common law world in Asia and Africa, though people are aware that socio-legal reality tends to be quite different. Somehow, there are mental blocks when it comes to identifying the internal plurality of law and making clear distinctions between different types of law. This shows that history has not taught us enough about the crucial messages contained in legal pluralism, a supposedly new theory which is actually an ancient theme, but was sidelined and ignored in the age of Enlightenment and the rush towards modernity.

From his armchair perspective, Sir Henry Maine had perceived the ancient Hindu texts as codes.[31] Maine was therefore at least willing to accept that Hindus were somewhat civilised people. Though they did many repugnant things, it was accepted, to the chagrin of the then ruling Muslims, that Hindus had their own laws. This realisation was important, because otherwise the colonial history of India might have developed quite differently, more like in parts of Africa, where the British assumed that the locals had no laws at all, and that civilisation thus needed to be brought to them, also in the shape of socio-legal norms. Images of a virtual *tabula rasa* or *terra nullius*, particularly in Africa and Australia, justified massive appropriation of property as well as prominent impositions in specific territories of English common law as it stood at a particular point of time.

Lawyers should have been aware that this particular process never occurred in India on a large scale.[32] The British themselves did not really introduce English law into India, as they could have done. English law was only imported for colonial staff in the major cities, not in the *mufassil*, the hinterland. Clearly, the British themselves did not want to be governed by local Muslim laws, the "official law" at the time of the British East India Company. But they did not really wish to go as far as imposing English law on their colonial subjects. From 1765 onwards, most clearly in the scheme established by Warren Hastings in 1772, the British recognised that there were different laws for different groups of people in India, based primarily on religious affiliation. Hence they divided the whole legal field into "general law", matters like criminal law, contract and commercial law, and "personal laws", basically matters of the family and of religion.

Much writing claims that the British invented and introduced the personal law system into India,[33] but that seems quite wrong. In reality, the personal law system is, if anything, an earlier Hindu institution or invention, reflecting the recognition of different forms of belief and practice among a large population which mostly gave crucial importance to local customs, as the early *smriti* texts clearly recognise. Therefore, early Christians, Jews, Parsis and later also Muslims could previously live under Hindu domination and follow their own personal law systems. Later local Muslim rulers, and then the Moghuls, also accepted the same system with some modifications and saw the advantages of cosmopolitan plurality, as current research reconfirms.[34] The British colonial structures, thus, were simply built as a kind of superstructure onto established pattern and fitted into the pre-existing Indian framework. Apart from adding some laws for themselves, the new rulers merely assimilated to the Indian legal environment and increased its legal diversity by their presence.

But the British eventually introduced significant changes to the legal structure as a whole when they codified what came to be called the general law, as planned by Hastings in 1772, so that India acquired the Indian Penal Code in 1860, the Indian Evidence Act of 1872 and the Indian Contract Act of the same year, plus many more enactments. In the realm of personal laws, however, very few legislative interventions were made, certainly not any form of comprehensive codification. Even the eventual British-inspired codifications of the general Indian law after 1860 were not simple transplants of existing English law, but instead carefully crafted complex new constructs, designed for use in a colonial territory rather than in England itself. The best example remains of course the Indian Penal Code of 1860, still in force all over the subcontinent, while England has even today no codified criminal law.

The deeply flawed assumption that ancient Hindu law had earlier been codified through the *!"stric* texts and was further codified through British colonial interventions is thus based on a series of incorrect lessons from Indian legal history. This befuddlement certainly misguided colonial and also later law reformers in India into believing that one could simply replace ancient Hindu codes with new secular rules. The same conceptual misunderstanding prevents many people today, scholars and common citizens alike, from making sense of the complex nature and structure of current Indian laws, and of the present place of Hindu law within this complex structure.[35] The prominent predilection for the ambitious agenda of secularisation through codifying law reform has its roots in such misconceptions and remains evidently as powerful as ever today, not only in India. Such uniform visions seem to cloud the mind when it comes to understanding the trajectory of India's post-modern uniform civil code agenda. While history remains relevant, its lessons about legal pluralism have manifestly not been fully learnt.

*****

V
Hindu Law and Religion as India's Dominant Systems in a Plural Context

Evidently, the mental image of legal codification also relates closely to global debates about religion and its relationship with law. The idea that Moses came down from Mount Sinai with God's commandments is familiar in most of the world. Centuries later, the claim that a man called Mohammad received God's law to pass on to the world, and especially to all those who were willing to accept this message, became an equally powerful symbol of the innate strength of religious law and the foundation for a new world religion. The worldwide spread of Christianity and Islam confirms that such powerful images of how humans are linked to the Universe constitute not only religious messages, but also contain powerful political, social and legal guidance, creating holistic systems of Truth and knowledge on which later man-made legal systems could be built.

Through this, the Pope came to be perceived as God's representative on earth and the Prophet of Islam became much more than a mere messenger. Through contact with divine authority, he gained personal authority and power, also in political, social and legal terms. Such a person then tends to become a leader, the first ruler, the man who effectively controls the law, because he alone had direct contact with the religious source. But as long as God remains the supervening force, such a human figure does not, indeed must not, become the dominant maker of law.[36] The later secularisation of law, also of Islamic law, could occur – of course not without much agonising - once natural law and positivism had become linked, making *siyasa shar'iyya* as Islamic "good governance" human and partly secular, while still religiously legitimised as a tool to implement and maintain the Law of God. Today, all legal systems, whether religious or state-centric, have come under global pressure to secularise (if not, now, internationalise), while there is also much countervailing pressure to localise and, indeed, often to Islamise.[37] Historically, Islamic law is therefore certainly not alone in resisting uniformity and modernising pressures; medieval Christian law once also resisted claims of the superiority of state law and various forms of resistance are also reported from Africa and elsewhere.[38]

India as an internally plural entity remains dominated by complex Indic forms of values, ethics and religions, with no agreement over what to call such religious phenomena as "Hinduism",[39] and where and how to draw boundaries. "Hinduism" is manifestly not a religion based on direct divine revelation through human agents. Its sources are largely chthonic,[40] but no less sophisticated than the ancient Greek models that underpin "Western" civilisation and "our" traditional concepts of natural law. There is no centralised belief system focused on one Hindu God, and yet there is the concept of a unifying linking force, overshadowed in the daily realities of life by polytheistic practices and beliefs and a plethora of local and sectarian manifestations of religion. We shall see in a moment how this relates to current legal realities in India.

While the concept of a monotheistic deity is certainly not absent in Hindu thought, the reality of polytheism and of a plurality of chosen deities clearly dominates the various Hindu cultures and societies, and thus the whole of India's socio-religious arena. There is no central figure of a Hindu Prophet as a special person, instead there were many Vedic sages (*rishis*) who are said to have "heard" the Vedic hymns in a process of revelation called *shruti*. Later generations then passed on this ancient knowledge through chains of human memory or remembrance (*smriti*), which is also the technical term for a huge class of ancient texts. Consequently, in Hinduism and Hindu law, it is not possible, as could be done with more success for Judaism, Christianity or Islam, to make a strong claim that there must be uniformity of belief and shared basic concepts of the religion. Very early on, thus, Hindus agreed to disagree and cultivated respect for internal diversity. Differently put, they refused to claim that humans could know precisely who God was, and instead admitted (as Christians and Muslims actually also do in their own ways) that it remains beyond human capacity to fully comprehend ultimate Truths. Thus, rather than constructing a religious doctrine of uniformity, Hinduism as India's majoritarian belief system allowed and developed a plurality-focused body of theory and of practice, which leads directly to the present confusing and messy picture of Hinduism as more of a collection of sects rather than one stratified religion. This also explains continued reliance on Hindu customary law, even in modern statutes, such as sections 7 and 29(2) of the Hindu Marriage Act of 1995 in relation to customary solemnisation of marriages and customary divorces. On top of this, the inability to neatly define a "Hindu" creates many fuzzy boundaries for determining allegiance to any particular personal law. The temptation to argue for one law for all Indians arises to some extent out of frustration about such messy diversities.

It is, however, often overlooked that Muslims and Christians, too, do not have internally uniform legal systems. Muslims have been arguing forever over the meaning and implications of certain Arabic words and expressions.[41] The Muslim concept of legal pluralism, *ikhtilaf* or "tolerated diversity of opinion", indicates that Islamic law can also be perceived as a holistically interlinked and internally plural system, so that there is no uniform Islamic law, just as there is no such thing as uniform Hindu law. The innate diversities of Hindu belief and practice meant that Hindus have often been treated as primitive, especially by those who rely on divine revelation. While Muslims accepted Christians, Jews and Parsis as people of the book (*kitabiyya*) and allowed themselves to marry women from those communities, they shunned so-called idol worshippers.[42] In response, many Hindus developed defensive strategies, some would say inferiority complexes, and have tried to claim that "Hinduism" has long had all the paraphernalia of other world religions. It appears that prominent thinkers of neo-Hinduism and later Hindu fundamentalism were partly incited by Muslim aggression,[43] an observation that remains true of Hindu nationalist tendencies among overseas Indians today.

In colonial times, Hindus tried to tell the British and others that their religion had a holy book, too, first of all the Veda.[44] Hindus as India's majority thus like to claim (apparently with considerable justification) that their system of religion and law is older than that of "the others", and certainly not inferior. Many Hindus also tend to claim there is one God, whether the more impersonal Brahma or *bhagwan*, or Krishna or Rama, an ideal ruler figure, who became a still more prominent Hindu deity partly through Ayodhya-inspired Hindu nationalism (*hindutva*).[45] In fact, the frequent argument now is that Hindu concepts should prevail in India because they constitute the intellectual property of the demographic majority. One can see how easily this line of reasoning turns the arguments in favour of a

Uniform Civil Code towards attempts to Hinduise the nation and to simply get rid of Muslim and Christian personal laws. The "fundamentalist" reasoning that India's future should be determined mainly or even exclusively by Hindu majoritarian concepts (more so while India had a Hindu nationalist government for a number of years until close to the millennium) certainly added some sobering realism and important reservations about the Uniform Civil Code debates towards the end of the twentieth century. But few Indian writers are discussing this openly, leaving Europeans and North Americans to fussy debates over the crisis of secularism in India.[46]

*****

VI
Learning To Respect Differences In Independent India

However, since that fateful time of Indian independence in mid-August 1947, it has become crystal-clear that India would have to be the home of all kinds of people and not just a Hindu state. This is exactly where the shoe pinches for many nervous observers. With only a slowly decreasing demographic majority of 85% to 80% Hindus, according to the Census figures of 2001, independent India will remain Hindu-dominated for a very long time. Minorities would probably face more difficulties if minority protection was not so securely anchored in the Indian Constitution.[47] The majoritarian Hindu law is not allowed by a plurality-conscious constitution to become the law of the land. The resulting process of postcolonial diversity-conscious Indian identity construction has been difficult, no doubt, but it has also brought some unexpected results, as the present article illustrates.

Scholars who argued vigorously in favour of a Uniform Civil Code have expressed frustrations about long "sterile debates" while voicing doubts about the possibility of its implementation.[48] Some prominent Indian legal scholars now privilege recourse to international values,[49] but local "identity postulates" would appear to be of necessity plural entities infused with local notions.[50] The problem with such writing that favours legal uniformity is that it seeks to minimise and belittle the influence of Hindu law, really of all personal laws, as a basis for Indian law making, while privileging state-made secular laws and even international law over the culturally-anchored laws of the people of India.[51]

How to deal legally with cultural differences is, of course, a global conundrum observed all over the world today, not just in India. On the level of ideology, emphasis on uniformity is employed to achieve conformity to some kind of dominant model, formally to the exclusion of other voices. Earlier, that formal model, often through colonialism, became perceived to be that of "the West", and for India this was more specifically thought to be the British model. So both coloniser and colonised assumed that there was a desirable advanced method by which a vast country could be run and administered coherently, a precursor to current global trends. We can easily see how, on a global level today, such kinds of tensions become even more inextricable.

During post-colonial reconstruction, with its reformist euphoria from the 1950s onwards, India was in danger of losing sight of its traditional respect for local and cultural difference.

After Independence in August 1947, India had several options, particularly the traditional decentralised, Hindu-centric Gandhian approach and the ebulliently modernist state-centric, secular approach of Dr. Ambedkar. Nehru found himself torn between these two poles. M.K. Gandhi wanted to emphasise the village, local cultures, customary norms, and thus legal plurality, focused on the self-controlled ordering systems of traditional Hindu *dharma*.[52] He thought that justice would be better served by taking account of the facts and circumstances of every case rather than following codified precedent. The modernists around Dr. Ambedkar preferred a strong central state with codified laws and as much legal uniformity as possible. While Gandhi was perceived as wanting a "return" to ancient religious and cultural models, the modernists wanted to "advance" and to follow "the West" as much as possible, abandoning the shackles of the past. Ambedkar in particular wanted to see a secular modern India with the same laws for all, a Western-style model like France or Germany, while others were bitterly opposed to this.[53] While the temptation to make India a Hindu-dominated state was present and to some extent embodied by Mahatma Gandhi, those in control, above all Nehru and the people around him, prevailed to set India on the road to a peculiar kind of secularism, unique to India and widely misunderstood or, rather, inadequately understood. In essence, Indian secularism means equidistance of the state from all religions. It is not based on a clear-cut division of law and religion, but recognises their holistic interconnections and seeks to guarantee minorities equal treatment in a Hindu-dominated new state.

Thus diversity-conscious realism prevailed over uniform ideology and the Indian Constituent Assembly soon got down to formulating India's new Constitution of 1950. Law reform was written into the national programme of development; the existing plurality of laws with the personal law system as a central element was now simply re-anchored within the overarching framework of the Indian Constitution. This presents an intricate compromise between uniformity and diversity, centrality and localism. Although the Constitution seems to Americans and others to be similar to the American Constitution, it is actually typically Indian, full of recognition of differences between various groups of people and respectful of diversity at many levels.[54]

There is reluctant admiration worldwide for the fact that this Constitution has been so successful in guiding India's massive democracy.[55] In my view much of that success must be attributed to this explicit basic structure of a compromise between uniformity and diversity.

Uniformity became a big issue in the formative debates. Ambedkar vigorously argued for a Uniform Civil Code as a secularising device, designed to get rid of Hindu law and of "tradition" altogether.[56] He was apparently less concerned about Muslim law. His project of uniformity and modernity failed, however, for good reason, apparently because the Indian leadership under Nehru realized already then that uniformity could not be decreed by the stroke of a pen. In the same way, more recent Hindu nationalist attempts to get rid of Muslim law through pushing the agenda of the Uniform Civil Code have also miserably collapsed, and respect for diversity has come out triumphant. As indicated, in 1950 the Uniform Civil Code was put on hold and instead, as a future agenda item, one of the many Directive Principles of State Police was planted as Article 44 into the Constitution. The Directive stated that "[t]he state shall endeavor to secure for the citizens a uniform civil code throughout the territory of India".[57]

But what did and do such words mean? A phrase like "shall endeavour to secure" reads like an admission that uniformisation would be a very difficult process, with no timetable given and no clear agenda beyond the eventual aim of greater uniformity. Purposely left vague, neither time-bound nor clearly defined, this has been seen by various authors as a provision that has no hope of being implemented, that is "no more than a distant mirage".[58] But significantly, these same words of Article 44 are still interpreted today by leading secularity-focused legal scholars of India as a binding programme for action.[59]

During the fierce debates about Hindu law codification in India in the 1950s, it became quite clear that even Hindu law as a whole was far too diverse internally to be subjected to a rigid process of uniformisation and codification. The various local and customary rules of Hindu law could not be fitted into a uniform Hindu law code, so the ambitious project of codification of Hindu law was abandoned early on. Instead four Acts were created in 1955 and 1956 to regulate selected aspects of Hindu law-the Hindu Marriage Act in 1955 and three further Acts on Hindu law in 1956. So in legal reality, India ended up, towards the mid-1950s, with a complex regime of Hindu law regulation which gave rise to most interesting litigation in years to come, but which was certainly not uniform at all. Buddhists, Jainas and Sikhs were also subsumed under Hindu law during this reform process.[60]

In addition, the personal laws of Muslims, Christians, Parsis and Jews, the option of using a secular legal regime, as provided under the Special Marriage Act of 1954, and many regional laws and amendments were largely left intact. Indian law, therefore, followed the familiar South Asian strategy of focusing primarily on reforms to the majority law while leaving the various minority laws untouched. The jungle of Indian family laws remained a dense forest.[61]

VII
The Persistence of Legal Differences In Modern India

Hence, after the initial decade of modernising Hindu law reforms in the 1950s, India remained a country, like almost all other nations in Asia and Africa, in which different personal laws for different groups of people were applied. A prominent illustration to critique this "backward" state of play, which is frequently cited, is that an Indian Muslim man could therefore, even today, marry up to four wives at the same time, while all other Indian men could have only one wife.[62] At least, that is the impression from the outside, studying only the statutory law and noting the absence of statutory regulation or control of polygamy in Indian Muslim law. Few people have had the time to study what happened and happens in socio-legal reality.[63] The inevitably prominent issue in Indian law became thus whether it was constitutionally valid to maintain such distinctions between Indian citizens merely on the basis of religion. Should citizens have vastly different rights and duties merely because they belonged to a particular religious community? Since the law could not abolish communities, could and should Indian law at least remove the discriminatory legal consequences of social and religious differences?

This matter has remained deeply controversial and has been most interestingly litigated in relation to the thorny issue of post-divorce maintenance for women under Indian law.

Following the much-cited and heavily misused *Shah Bano* case of 1985,[64] which even many people in the West claim to know about (though they may know nothing else about Indian law), the eventual verdict of the Indian Supreme Court in *Danial Latifi* in 2001 merely reiterated the existing legal position, namely that making reasonable distinctions between citizens on the basis of certain criteria, in this case religion, would not be unconstitutional in itself.[65]

Not surprisingly, however, between the 1950s and 2001, the debates about the Uniform Civil Code in India, and on legal uniformity in general, have continued to be lively. While the old Gandhian/Nehruvian dichotomy has never gone away, the discourse took various forms at different times, depending on the politics of the day and new developments in the law. At first, the demands of modernisation, leading to globalisation, led towards a belief that modern India needed to follow the West, particularly perhaps Britain. My predecessor in London, Professor Derrett, argued vigorously in 1957,[66] and until the early 1970s, that when it came to family law reforms, India could do no better than copying English family law and following the steps of modernisation taken in London. This advice was less geared towards uniformity than somewhat culture-blind modernisation, despite Derrett's deep insights into Hindu law and Indian legal traditions. However, Professor Derrett's views began to change after reading Indian cases about the effects of the new regime of Hindu divorce law after a 1964 amendment.[67] This new Act assumed gender equality but made it easier for Hindu men to throw their wives out of the marriage, and out of the house, even against their will, thereby engineering a unilateral divorce which led to what Derrett called the "own wrong problem".[68] Prevented from entering the house every time they tried to come back, frequently beaten with polluting leather sandals (*chappals*), wives were simply expelled from the matrimonial home when the husband stated that, as far as he was concerned, the marriage had broken down. Derrett's acute realisation that failure to take account of cultural factors in the application of family laws could cause unforeseen social disasters in a patriarchally dominated legal system is documented in his last book on Hindu family law.[69] After noting that the Marriage Laws (Amendment) Act of 1976 had resulted in still more amazingly gender-insensitive case law, the grand master retired. Thereafter, when the Indian state wanted to introduce further divorce law reforms in 1981, including the principle of "irretrievable breakdown", a concept borrowed from English law, even Indian women's groups rose in opposition and the Bill was defeated.

Although India stopped copying English legal developments in matrimonial law around 1981, when I came into the field I was immediately confronted with the havoc caused in Indian society by these modernising and uniformising Indian family law reforms. It had become possible for an Indian husband to enjoy the "first night" after a traditional wedding, to claim next morning that something was wrong with her, and to demand virtually instant nullity. Any excuse or minor blemish would become a legal ground to terminate the marriage.[70] It was frightening; women were given no chance to plead their side of the story. North Indian judges, in particular, would simply decree divorce even though irretrievable breakdown did not exist on the statute book.

Such grave social and legal consequences of unthinking modernisation in the realm of Hindu family law gradually made many Indian judges rethink their strategies of dealing with family conflicts. Blind modernisation came to be seen as undesirable from about 1988 onwards.[71] A more careful approach was gradually, but by no means systematically, taken. Considering more specifically the facts and circumstances of each case, courts now sought to ensure that women and children should not be disadvantaged by liberal divorce laws, since it was obvious that men could often afford better lawyers and exploit unfair advantages.

Thus, Indian judges in several High Courts and the Supreme Court, but not Parliament, became the main motor for important gradual, almost imperceptible, legal developments which also impacted the question of the Uniform Civil Code. The shift to the judicial arena and expansion of the judicial domain is not unique to family law, falling in line with scholars' observations of a general judicialisation, if not emerging juristocracy, in Indian law.[72] It is highly significant in the present context that not primarily problems of gender difference, but more specifically the economic consequences of their decisions made Indian judges rethink the implications of judicial interventions in family law.[73] Since India does not have, and will most probably not develop, a Western-style welfare state, it became necessary to embark on a major restructuring of family law policies, especially regarding access to divorce and maintenance provisions after divorce.

During this period, one can observe a subtle gradual shift away from dogged demands for a Uniform Civil Code and uniform legal regulation for all Indians towards a system in which justice as a relative matter (*ny"ya*) reasserted itself. Of course, there were still quite prominent cases in which courts criticised the absence of a Uniform Civil Code.[74] Surprisingly, this kind of argument could still be heard even after 2001.[75]

Such cases may still cause catchy headlines, but are becoming rarer now, though some older Indian academics still enthusiastically propagate legal uniformity as a desirable aim for India today.[76]

There are many indications that most Indian judges have now become post-modern realists the hard way. Thus, significantly, it has been held that where a litigating couple is desperately poor, the husband or wife could not be expected by the law to maintain the other; both parties would have to suffer this misfortune together.[77]

Where, on the other hand, one spouse is significantly better placed than the other, that spouse, normally the man, has a legal obligation to share his wealth.[78] While modern Hindu law, in its enthusiasm for modernity, also introduced the gender-equal rule that a wife might have to maintain the husband if she is better placed than him,[79] Hindu men who have tried to argue that they should be maintained by their wife have been told to exert themselves and to work for their family. Such men are virtually ridiculed by the courts,[80] unless they are disabled and reliant on the support of others.

The main new message of uniformity, then, is that all Indian men, as controllers of most of the property and resources in India, are primarily liable for the welfare of any wives and children in need of support. Full gender equality in copied Western garb is not quite what India has been seeking to achieve, nor would it sensible. A culture-specific re-appraisal of moral responsibility was increasingly turned into emphasis on the legal obligation of males to maintain family members by the quiet activism or occasional deliberate passivism of the Indian judiciary.

*****

VIII
Contribution Of The Legislature In Interaction with Courts

Significantly, the Indian legislature has followed suit, most recently by promulgation of the Maintenance and Welfare of Parents and Senior Citizens Act, 2007, which is not the subject of the present article, but is also a uniform social welfare law applying to all Indians. The new dominant concern for social welfare principles in India strongly relies on ancient principles of responsibility within the family context. It had earlier been re-imported into the new Criminal Procedure Code of 1973, which ominously defined a "wife" as including a divorced wife but made no immediate impact.[81] But because that Code applies to all Indians, it now became possible for Muslim wives to ask for maintenance beyond the traditional *iddat* period of three months, basically to ask for lifelong maintenance. This is what set the ball of Indian post-modern legal developments rolling and contributed critically, as we shall see presently, to the new pattern of harmonised personal laws.

The famous *Shah Bano* case eventually surfaced from this legal issue.[82] After almost 40 years of marriage and several children, an elderly Muslim woman was thrown out by her lawyer husband so that he could enjoy life with a younger woman. He claimed that giving his old former wife the stipulated *iddat* money and the dower (*haq mahr*), together just a few hundred Indian Rupees, fulfilled his legal obligations towards her, relying on traditional Muslim law to exempt himself from any further liability. Well before the *Shah Bano* case, however, the increasingly activist Indian Supreme Court had already established in a 1979 case that a Muslim ex-husband would only be exempt from further payments to his ex-wife if the payments were sufficient for her "to keep body and soul together".[83] The legislature had evidently laid sound foundations for this kind of judicial activist approach in the Criminal Procedure Code of 1973.

Thus, India's important social welfare considerations were introduced by a combination of judicial activism and legislative alertness to assist divorced Muslim wives against vagrancy and destitution. When Shah Bano's husband engineered his case to get around the social welfare argument by the Supreme Court, the judges of the Supreme Court, incidentally five Hindu judges, struck back and held, quite rightly, that even under certain Qur'anic provisions, there was an obligation on a divorcing Muslim husband to be considerate and generous to his former wife.[84]

In this manner, the *Shah Bano* case acted as a catalyst for post-modern Indian legal developments in more recent statute law that scholars and other observers have found immensely difficult to unravel. Of course, this case and the 1986 Act protecting the rights of divorced Muslim wives created enormous political outcry, at first among Muslims, later also among secularists. Initial concern about maintenance for divorced Muslim wives was soon overshadowed by the politicised football of the Uniform Civil Code, on which the judges had pronounced towards the end of the *Shah Bano* judgment, which caused widespread riots and protests. Even *India Today*, a leading news magazine and apparently a major source of knowledge among overseas and other middle class Indians about Indian law, has not yet understood the intricacies of this episode. Relying on political gossip rather than legal analysis, journalists and even serious academics continue to engineer curious misunderstandings and serious misinformation about legal facts.[85]

Such problems of perception and insight are centrally relevant to the present discussion and thus require some further explanation. As just noted, we still frequently read of how Rajiv Gandhi quickly gave in to the rioting Muslims after the *Shah Bano* case and in record time made an Act, the Muslim Women (Protection of Rights on Divorce) Act of 1986, which took away all rights of divorced Muslim wives to maintenance from their former husbands.[86] Thus, suiting the more strongly emerging Hindu nationalist argumentation, the dominant allegation became that Muslim men were once more given exceptional privileges (in addition to permission to be polygamous) by the modern

Indian state on the basis of religious exemption. Fortunately for India, this has turned out to be politicised gossip, cleverly engineered misinformation. Not only is this loved by the press, but also many scholars and other people around the world uncritically continue to use such convenient fictions, because they seem to show so convincingly that the Indian state (or rather the Congress Party, to be more precise in this political cauldron) is continuing to give excessive favours to Muslims. Closely linked to this is the argument that it would be much better to implement a Uniform Civil Code, so that such communal politicking would become impossible. Clearly, the agenda of many commentators had become the abolition of Indian Muslim personal law through merging it into the Uniform Civil Code. Many modernist scholars unwittingly supported the agenda of Hindu nationalists, which explains some of the embarrassed silence around the present topic.

As we are now gradually realizing, legal reality was quite different, but many observers still find the truth incredible, because the myths created around the *Shah Bano* saga remain so powerful. As a matter of hard fact, no financial upper limit for post-divorce maintenance payments was laid down by the Indian legislature in the 1986 Act.[87] This clearly meant that Indian Muslim husbands were not only principally held liable for the future welfare of their ex-wives, but faced a potentially much higher and hence clearly discriminatory burden, since all other Indian ex-husbands might have to pay only up to 500 Rupees per month to an ex-wife. But nobody noticed this in the heat of the arguments. Everybody, including for some time myself, thought that Rajiv Gandhi had indeed caved in to Muslim demands. So despite murmurs of disapproval about the 1986 Act, there were no Muslim riots on the street after this Act was passed. Clearly, the legislative ploy had worked, in that everyone was told (and was happy to believe) that divorcing Muslim men had no further legal responsibility for their ex-wives after the *iddat* period. The result of that perception was, of course, that modernists and secularists were now vigorously complaining that the Indian state had violated Article 44 of the Constitution by making a new personal status law specifically for Muslims.

Loud claims were made (and curiously continue to be made in the global literature) about the fact that the Indian state allegedly let down all divorced Muslim wives.[88]

All of this has meanwhile turned out to be a textbook case of scholarly fiction and confused politicised gossip. In fact, as we now know from the Indian Supreme Court's verdict in *Danial Latifi* in 2001, Indian Muslim wives have all along been protected by the *Shah Bano* precedent (which was confirmed as good law in 2001), as well as by the provisions of the 1986 Act itself, which were firmly defended as constitutionally valid.

In fact, we had quite subtly been told all of this much earlier by the Indian Supreme Court, carefully testing the waters through skilfully engineered *obiter dicta* in some other cases,[89] but nobody wanted to believe this. It also seems now that nobody was supposed to understand this fully until the right moment came in global history, two weeks after 9/11, to present these facts to the nation in an authoritative Supreme Court decision, the *Danial Latifi* case. So all along, it had been the law that Muslim ex-husbands under the 1986 Act, like all Indian ex-husbands under the provisions of s. 125 of the Criminal Procedure Code of 1973, had remained liable throughout for the welfare of their ex-wife until they had made adequate provisions for the woman's survival at a level appropriate to the parties.

While this was certainly not the officially distributed version, and was definitely not what the press and "activist" human rights watchers picked up from this controversy, this politically difficult and potentially dangerous conclusion (specifically in terms of another Muslim backlash of riots, or worse) had earlier been gradually documented by an increasing number of reported High Court cases. These have existed in reported form since about 1988, with particular strength and elaborate arguments in the Kerala High Court.[90] But who reads Indian High Court cases!? So the law of India - gradually, but unnoticed - had clearly begun to be that all Indian ex-husbands, including Muslim men, would have to pay maintenance to their ex-wives until they die or remarry. There was no escape route. Under the special provisions of the new 1986 Act, as noted, Muslim husbands actually found with few exceptions that they were now subjected to a tougher regime of responsibility, since there were no upper financial limits. Also the courts began to watch more closely that actions should be more strictly time-bound.

Under section 3 of the 1986 Act, then, as interpreted progressively by the High Courts in dozens of reported cases, not only did a Muslim ex-husband have to maintain the ex-wife during the *iddat* period (which any decent Muslim should do anyway, but many fail to do), but within that time period he also had to "make and pay" provisions for the time after the *iddat* period. In other words, if a Muslim divorced wife reached the end of her *iddat* period and the husband had not maintained her and had not made reasonable provisions for her future welfare (which might include arranging a remarriage for her), the ex-wife could go to court once the *iddat* finished and could claim both entitlements. I have seen for myself in South India how effectively this may assist women in bargaining for their rights within the family.

At the same time, I am aware of the rightful criticism that going to court to enforce one's entitlements remains a major problem for most women in India, perhaps especially for lower middle class Muslim ex-wives claiming their rights under the 1986 Act.[91] Justice, indeed, is not just delivered on a silver platter. But the new laws have contributed enormously to women's empowerment in this field. Meanwhile, there are more recently reported cases which raise questions over Muslim women who claim potentially unfair benefits, so that some men, again in Kerala, have quite rightly begun to ask the courts for re-assessing gender justice.[92]

*****

IX
Towards Legal Uniformity Despite Personal Laws

Worse for India's Muslim husbands, as already noted in passing, was that while the Criminal Procedure Code of 1973 had fixed an upper limit of 500 Rupees, there were no financial limits for the ex-wife's entitlements under the 1986 Act for Muslims. Thus, under this new dispensation, everything depended now on the financial circumstances of the spouses. Indeed there is a case, notably again from Kerala, where a Muslim woman who already had a million Rupees wanted more money from her millionaire husband, and she was successful.[93] No riots followed this decision, either. It appears that this further re-assured the faraway Delhi lawmakers (who appear to have been watching this carefully) that the climate was eventually beginning to be right for more steps to secure better financial protection for all Indian women.

Unnoticed by virtually all legal scholars and other observers, thus, legal uniformity in this particular area of Indian law has come in through the back door, or as a reflection of the moon in a mirror held up to an obviously patriarchal society. While Indian Muslims had earlier used so-called religious arguments to escape from the official Indian social welfare regime with its basic rule that in a patriarchal society, men should be primarily responsible for the welfare of women and children, this argument has badly backfired. India's judges as gatekeepers of the Indian welfare system firmly cajoled such Muslim sharks back into the post-modern Indian net of social welfare arrangements. That welfare system is clearly not built on direct state-made support as in Western countries, but was cleverly designed to ensure that families look after attached individuals and, more specifically, that men remain responsible for the welfare of their ex-wives and children.

As the judicial interpretations of the 1986 Act show, and certainly after *Danial Latifi* in 2001,94 it seems now that the Indian state bureaucracy realised that they should sacrifice, or rather de-prioritise, the principle of formal legal uniformity if the higher object of securing equitable legal entitlements can be achieved in other ways – even more so if this is fiscally prudent. Thus, it was apparently decided that Indian Muslims can have or keep their specific personal laws if they want them and insist on them, but they cannot claim exemption from social welfare obligations that apply uniformly to all Indians. It seems therefore that the uniformised post-modern Indian law has begun to incorporate some benign elements of traditional *shari'a* law which today's patriarchal South Asian Muslims and their jurists (guided to some extent by leading Muslim scholars like Tahir Mahmood) may not fully wish to accept. In fact, this would not be the first time that a principle of Muslim law has become adopted elsewhere in Indian law.[95]

As noted, the *Danial Latifi* decision and its manifestly pro-women approach in forcing Muslim men to make appropriate arrangements for the future maintenance of their ex-wives, did not cause any riots on the streets of India at the time. However, it has also not been debated fully enough, as sharply noted by one of the major commentators on current developments in Indian gender justice.[96]

A deeper reason for this studied silence appears to be that the decision in *Danial Latifi* represents a defeat for legal modernism as much as for traditional Muslims. It is therefore also embarrassing to most positivism-focused legal scholars. It is evident, though, that the almost stunned reception of this verdict swiftly cleared the road for an alert government to make two further significant piecemeal enactments in related areas to smoothen the path towards greater legal uniformity in Indian family law.

Hardly noticed so far, a further path-breaking legal development in Indian family laws occurred only two days after the decision in *Danial Latifi*, on 24 September 2001, when Act 50 of 2001, the Code of Criminal Procedure (Amendment) Act of 2001, was passed. The impact of this small but highly significant piece of legislation is making itself felt by 2007, as more women and other disadvantaged family members realize that they have legal rights against men who control the family property.[97] Since no easily available explanation of legislative intent was offered,[98] the question remains whether this is purposeful silence, legislation by stealth, or a planned new strategy to reinstate a higher level of legal uniformity.

It is evident, though, that this particular Act cannot be an accident and that it does three important things at once. Firstly, the Act simply removed the earlier ceiling for maintenance of 500 Rupees in section 125(1) of the Criminal Procedure Code of 1973 for all Indians. This reinstates legal uniformity in the level of liability to maintain ex-wives for all Indian ex-husbands. This has resulted in litigation by wives and relatives of the middle class, not just at the lowest levels of society as before, where vagrancy and homelessness were central issues. Secondly, the 2001 Act introduces a new proviso to strengthen rights to maintenance *pendente lite* or interim maintenance, given that so many claimants suffer because of tardy implementation of laws in this field.[99] Thirdly, and closely linked, this law promises in another proviso speedy disposal of such cases, as far as possible, within sixty days from the date of the service of notice.

I suggest that we must take these new provisions seriously, even if their implementation will take time, and will probably never be perfect. After all, this is India, where state law is only one type of law that people may use. The Indian state, however, appears to mean business here, though people will need time learning to use (and as always, abuse) this new law. There will also be much resistance.

I fear, for example, that some more Indian women may be killed in so-called "dowry-related" murders if they make claims to financial support that are seen as unacceptable. Above all, judicial alertness will be needed to implement the undoubtedly beneficial Indian legal provisions on post-divorce maintenance, which may well be some kind of symbolic legislation. This is bound to have a deep impact on how gender relations are negotiated in Indian society today and will develop in the future. This significant legal reform shows the way for a gender-sensitive re-alignment of responsibilities of Indian family members to each other, remaining within a patriarchal context, which no amount of state law can abolish. While this type of law seems based on quite different assumptions than other recent laws made by the Indian Parliament, such as the Hindu Succession (Amendment) Act, 2005, which seems to privilege individual property rights, other recent enactments have again reinforced the liability of individuals for close family members.[100]

Most relevant for the present discussion on Indian legal uniformity is thus that the protective legal framework first created for Muslim ex-wives under the 1986 Act has now been further extended to all Indian ex-wives. Virtual legal uniformity has now been successfully reinstated after the 1986 Muslim personal law detour, though formally the relevant law is found in the amended 1973 Code and in the 1986 Act. In substance, there is no difference any more, but the identity of the personal law structure has been preserved.

The story of the gradual extension of such activist protection to all Indian citizens in need is thus a textbook example of the continuing power of activist and progressive personal law enactment in Indian law, ultimately designed to strengthen protection of individual rights, national cohesion and legal uniformity, in that order of importance. Indian men might well feel now that they are all, irrespective of religion and personal laws, in the same perilous boat. Getting married under Indian law now clearly means (as of course it did before) that men take on serious responsibilities for women and children, potentially for life, whether the marriage lasts or not. Thus, in an unexpected way the agendas of uniform nation building and support for traditional marriage arrangements have been conflated, leading to what some commentators have long seen as oppression of Indian men,[101] a topic on which much more may need to be said soon.

*****

X
Supporting Evidence from Growing Uniformity of Indian Divorce Laws

An equally telling example for the gradual move towards a uniform Indian family law system that retains the personal law structure while implementing legal equality across the personal law spectrum comes from recent developments in Indian divorce law, specifically concerning Indian Christian law. This personal law, earlier codified in the Indian Divorce Act of 1869 and the Indian Christian Marriage Act of 1872, used to be hopelessly outdated and in need of reform.

The Christian divorce law was originally promulgated at a time when divorce was granted with utmost reluctance and only in the most exceptional circumstances, mainly because of "religious" opposition from the Churches. After the liberalising reforms of Hindu divorce law in 1976, similar secularising reforms were introduced into Parsi divorce law in 1988.

Muslim *shari'a* law permits fairly easy divorce of either spouse, while favouring the husband's *talaq*, the traditional Muslim unilateral divorce formula of 'I divorce you'.[102] Christian divorce law, therefore, eventually came to stick out as discriminatory and thus unconstitutional.

Virtually imprisoning Christian spouses in unhappy marriages while allowing everyone else easier exit routes, this law cried out for modernisation, but Parliament did not act for decades.

Until recently, a Christian wife in particular was virtually chained into a marriage for ever, while her co-citizens of other religions could seek divorce when required.

Under the Constitution of India and its equality provisions, that was clearly a case which demonstrated the need for a Uniform Civil Code. But instead of asking Parliament to produce a Uniform Civil Code and thus offering Christian women the mixed blessings of an easy divorce regime, India's judges had already given up on Parliament which was seen as too busy with its own politicking. By 1995, after several unsuccessful attempts, the High Court of Kerala finally experimented with an alternative form of bringing about legal uniformity, removing certain restrictive words from section 10 of the old Indian Divorce Act of 1869, so that an Indian Christian wife could now seek divorce on the grounds of cruelty, like any other Indian citizen.[103] This daring step of judicial lawmaking never ceases to surprise my students in London, until they learn about India's public interest litigation and the various forms of judicial activism in the subcontinent. Through this skilful simple process of admittedly radical legal intervention, significantly again in Kerala, and restricted to that state until 2001, greater legal uniformity was achieved while keeping the personal law system intact.

Parliament eventually got the message that legislative action for the whole of India was overdue, but waited for the right time to reclaim the initiative in law making. It is perhaps no coincidence again that, only two days after the *Danial Latifi* case had been decided, on 24 September 2001, the Indian Parliament thus also passed the Indian Divorce (Amendment) Act, 2001 (Act No. 51 of 2001). This Act finally addressed the long-standing complaint that Christian spouses, particularly Christian women, were disadvantaged in access to divorce. The 2001 amendment has now brought Indian Christian divorce law broadly into line with the other divorce laws of India under the various personal laws and the largely optional provisions of the secular Special Marriage Act of 1954. Again, we see how legal harmonisation was achieved while retaining the personal law structure.

The new Act provides in section 10 ten grounds for dissolution of marriage among Christians, plus an additional ground for the wife if she can prove that "the husband has, since the solemnization of the marriage, been guilty of rape, sodomy or bestiality".[104] Some lawyers and activists in India, especially in the South, had fought long and hard for these amendments, which clearly represent another piece of the jigsaw puzzle of Indian legal uniformity that is now in place after enormously long lobbying and many setbacks.

*****

XI
Conclusion

In the West we clearly struggle with handling the various old and new challenges of cultural diversity, particularly now concerning "ethnic implants" introduced into our legal systems by massive migrations from Asia and Africa.[105] Interestingly, India seems to have found a harmonious solution to handle such age-old cultural diversities and the resulting pluralism of personal laws, leaving various strategic spaces for diversity when it matters, while controlling other spaces more strictly. In light of the evidence presented here, there can be no doubt that the post-modern Indian state has been systematically engaged in a fundamental restructuring of the country's social welfare laws, related to securing at least minimal strategic support for those citizens who are dependent on others. The state has done so in the intersection of criminal law and family law, killing two birds with one stone, as it were. While making the various personal laws more uniform and holding men across the board more explicitly accountable for the welfare of women, children, and now senior citizens, post-modern Indian law uses criminal law techniques to enforce social obligations. It seems that these agendas are more important to the Indian state now than the politics of personal law.

The newly activated social welfare orientation of the modern Indian state has thus relegated the political football of the Uniform Civil Code to a minor place on the league table of agendas. Notably, Indian law has not demanded full state control of marriages and does not require the formal registration of most marriages. With few exceptions (marriages involving foreigners, in particular) the solemnisation of marriages in India remains, across the board, a matter for society and customs, for clans, families and the concerned individuals, not for an inefficient state bureaucracy. At the same time, matters of financial security for wives and children appear to have become more important to the Indian state than the more explicitly political and high-profile issue of legal uniformity or the formal detail of marriage registration. Europeans of course tend to find this unsystematic and baffling, to say the least, and are tempted to view lack of formal state control as inefficient and proof of India's backwardness.

More deeply analysed, though, the Indian welfare state is shown here to be highly sophisticated in regulating this messy field through a plethora of informal devices like applying presumptions of marriage rather than insisting on formal documentation and empowering women through granting them statutory rights to maintenance. Of course, in the arena of maintenance law, the Indian state is now simply saving itself from welfare claims by its own disadvantaged citizens, throwing the welfare burden back to the claimant's family to save its own coffers, promising access to justice to people who need the support of the courts. A post-modern state can only use such strategies if it has not totally abandoned and legislated away the various aspects of traditional legal systems and their socio-cultural frameworks of values. It can only re-invent and re-utilise *dharma*, *sadacara* (good behaviour), *izzat* (honour and status in society) and other related concepts to rescue the desperately poor, abandoned, or divorced wives and other citizens if it is willing to co-opt "tradition". It seems that this is exactly what has happened in India. This also explains why there is so much embarrassed and partly annoyed silence concerning these new legal developments in post-modern India. A lot of modernist and secular observers are simply miffed about India's refusal to become "modern", and they may also be baffled by these new developments. At any rate, their silence is quite remarkable.

The integrated social welfare reforms in India that I analysed here raised important gender-related concerns. Existing dependencies on overwhelmingly male agents of control over resources will probably continue to prevail in most parts of the world, whatever gender-sensitive, equalising reforms are contemplated as even modern Western laws have not fully removed and curtailed patriarchy and gender discrimination. They have only managed to remove some glaring discrepancies and the most direct forms of discrimination. The Indian state, it seems, does not believe in aggressive gender revolution but prefers subtle strategies of diversity-sensitive evolution. That this movement towards a better future is perceived as too slow by many impatient activists is quite evident, but the post-modern Indian state is concerned with remaining realistic and is clearly nervous about causing riots and upheaval. So the Indian state does not officially promise its citizens the moon, knowing that the state would only be able to deliver a somewhat modified reflection of the desired object. I also see signs (particularly from many judgments) that government agencies in India realize that the social welfare promises of Western states have not been fully implemented and are now, to some extent, regretted, not the least because of mounting bills and spiraling costs. It would be worth examining those cases in detail.

Thus, realistically accepting patriarchy and informality as a fact, which is hardly a difficult task for Indian lawmakers - though it hurts the idealist feelings of many activists – seems to have become a newly invigorated *Grundnorm* for Indian law today. However, before male chauvinists rejoice too loudly, let us note that the flipside of this post-modern coin becomes that domineering men are now increasingly legally and not just morally obligated to use their discretionary superior control over wealth and resources within families for the benefit of *all* family members, so that no welfare burden is placed on society and/or on the state. Postmodern constitutional *dharma* in India, hardly a new item in the tool box, now relies again on self-controlled ordering within the traditional joint family network. This means today that men who hold the position of manager (*karta*) and control the purse strings of a family have to be actively involved in social welfare for those who depend on their financial support.

I can firmly conclude, therefore, that the Indian state has, certainly since 2001, become much clearer about the ultimate desired outcome of developmental agenda: Constitutional directives demand avoidance of a scenario in which millions of women, children and now the elderly are destitute, living on the road or the pavement of major cities, hungry, thirsty, and desperate for survival. This overriding agenda item is now clearly confirmed by the promulgation of India's amazing Maintenance and Welfare of Parents and Senior Citizens Act of 2007.

All of this means that the postmodern Indian state has learnt that welfare obligations are most definitely not a matter for direct control by the Indian state. They are not tasks which state agencies could reasonably and realistically fulfill. The state has thus again learnt to delegate obligations to society, a historical lesson that was never really forgotten. Since in India the number of welfare claimants under any category would be enormous, fiscal prudence, as much as a desire to protect women, children and the elderly, demands that a delegated approach to social welfare had to be chosen. It took postcolonial India several decades to implement this in a complex interplay of eventually post-modern statutes and case law, learning useful lessons along the way about sustainability of social welfare schemes that assumedly rich European nations are painfully tackling at the moment. German pensioners, to take only one example, are faced today with reduced commitments by the welfare state to pay for their medicines, complex operations, and many other entitlements that well-off citizens in rich nations seem to have become used to. They are often deeply disappointed with such developments, even though they may be rather well off. India, and quite rightly so, never wants to get into these kinds of problems in the first place by promising citizens too much as part of the social contract.

While such critical matters of social welfare have moved centre-stage, the case for the introduction of a Uniform Civil Code has continually become less prominent and less urgent. In fact, the agenda of uniform legislation has become far less convincing, more so since the continuing personal law system demonstrates that it can take care of the pressures of potential inequality through the intricate process of gradual harmonisation of all Indian personal laws and supervision by criminal and constitutional laws. It also helps the Indian post-modern state that the various personal law systems act as ethnic identifiers of India's celebrated unity in diversity. Thus in my view, India today, evidently more noticeably since those fateful weeks in September 2001, has achieved the equivalent of a Uniform Civil Code, which has clearly not taken the shape that the lawmakers of the 1940s first envisaged. The agenda have been reshuffled, but not totally changed, priorities have been re-adjusted, but the nation prospers, and vulnerable individuals are better protected than before.

Legal and scholarly debates, however, still lag seriously behind the actual development of the law, both in statutory and case law form. These new laws with their fine-tuned recognition of plurality make deep sense. I have always had problems with the political and legal ideology of total uniformity of laws as I always found the suggestion that a new uniform family law should or could be created by Parliament for all Indians totally unworkable in practice. Formally enforced legal uniformity can hardly lead to the situation-specific justice that the systems of *dharma, ny"ya and shariat* in their idealistic ambitions all sought and seek to achieve. It seems that India can indeed operate a formally uniform national legal system, like the

Constitution and much of the general law, but the "living law" itself, and particularly family law, will always remain culture-specific to a large extent, and thus marked by differentiations. Asking for a Uniform Civil Code in the simplistically uniform style desired by the law makers of the 1950s was therefore indeed like asking for the moon. Today, India can show those who still expect to see a uniform family law the mirror image of harmonised personal laws, as Mother Yashoda once did with little Krishna. That, in my view, is all that can be achieved by a diversity-conscious state through the agenda of uniform statutory law reform, even if it formally leaves out almost the entire field of Indian Muslim personal law.

The challenge now is to make the existing personal laws work better for as many Indians as possible in socio-legal reality, within the protective framework of the Indian Constitution. This is indeed a huge challenge in every respect, but this problem is by no means unique to Indian law. The lessons that India can draw from its scenario of continued plurality will be of much relevance to legal scholarship worldwide as well as governments, and clearly not only in Asia and Africa. If in Europe, legal systems can now increasingly accept non-traditional forms of marriage as legally recognised unions, for example, there is no sensible reason why other diversity-conscious arrangements could not be made.

It seems to me, however, that the key agenda item in all of this is not really or mainly cultural or ethnic diversity, but more the extent and firmness of state control. In other words, the critical element is positivism and its voracious appetite for demanding control of our lives. In the mainly legocentric Western legal systems, there is normally a dominant expectation of ultimate state control. Thus, states feel entitled to demand evidence of formal marriage registration and refuse to recognise any other marital arrangements and authorities as legitimising agents. Indian law shows, however, that demanding state registration of all marriages continues to be perceived as unrealistic. I suggest that this is not evidence of lack of development, but rather confirmation of India's sophistication in handling cultural diversity and legal pluralism.

The evidence is best illustrated by the well-considered refusal of India to introduce compulsory marriage registration. After certain recent high-profile calls by some Supreme Court judges for compulsory registration of all marriages in India, the Compulsory Registration of Marriages Bill of 2006 was put before Parliament as a Private Member Bill by a female *Rajya Sabha* (Upper House) member, Mrs. Vanga Geetha. The Bill portrays itself effortlessly as a magic wonder drug for getting rid of child marriages, polygamy, and women's legal insecurity regarding marital status. However, it has been sitting on the shelf of

Parliament for many, many months now, while other significant Acts, like the Prohibition of Child Marriage Act of 2006, have meanwhile become law.

If we check a little more carefully, we find the following dramatic legocentric flaw in this demand for the moon: Section 5 of the 2006 Bill suggests that "the marriage performed after the commencement of this Act shall be null and void if not registered within sixty days of solemnization of marriage". I think this particular wording alone explains why this Bill will not become an Act in India. It would cause havoc in Indian society to have such a law on the statute book.

Particularly in family law in any legal system, the systemic interplay of uniformity and plurality reflects the multiple realities of human life. I would argue that a good law should be about "the good life", about which we do not all have the same visions. Not everyone wants to get married. How do we then draw the precise boundaries between various forms of relationship and a legally recognised marriage?

Indian law appears to be deeply aware that total state control in this field is not only unrealistic, but ultimately wrong and immoral, because abusers of law and of people will seek to rely on formal rules to claim advantage over weaker persons.

Perhaps, thus, diversity-conscious respect for difference and its legal recognition is a better strategy for achieving justice than the blindfolded Eurocentric and simply modernist desire to get rid of difference and diversity altogether by means of legal reform.

*****

REFERENCES

1. Werner Menski, Comparative Law In A Global Context: The Legal Systems Of Asia And Africa, 4 (2d Ed. 2006).

2. Werner Menski, *Asking for the Moon: Legal Uniformity in India from a Kerala Perspective*, KERALA LAW TIMES, 2006(2), at 52.

3. Narmada Khodie, Readings In Uniform Civil Code (1975); Tahir Mahmood, An Indian Civil Code And Islamic Law (1976); Vasudha Dhagamwar, Towards The Uniform Civil Code (1989).

4. Shah Bano is an old Indian Muslim lady then in her seventies, now deceased, whose affluent lawyer husband famously deserted her for a younger woman and then sought to rely on traditional Muslim law to refuse any further responsibility for her welfare. *See* Mohd Ahmed Khan v. Shah Bano Begum, A.I.R. 1985 S.C. 945.

5. SATVINDER JUSS, INTERNATIONAL MIGRATION AND GLOBAL JUSTICE, 1 (2006) (discussing the idea that the world order today depends, to some extent, on freedom of movement).

6. New Work From Some Family Lawyers Is Beginning To Reflect This Concept. *Compare* Jon Murphy, Ethnic Minorities, Their Families And The Law (2000) *And* Jon Murphy, International Dimensions In Family Law, 2005) *With* Prakash

Shah, Law And Ethnic Plurality: Socio-Legal Perspectives (2007).

7. MENSKI, *supra* note 1, at 58.

8. WERNER MENSKI, Rethinking Legal Theory in Light of South-North Migration, in MIGRATION, DIASPORAS AND LEGAL SYSTEMS IN EUROPE 13-28 (Prakash Shah & Werner Menski eds., 2006.)

9. The voice of Buoaventura de Souza Santos has been particularly powerful in this respect. BUOAVENTURA DE SOUZA SANTOS, TOWARD A NEW LEGAL COMMON SENSE (2d ed. 2002); MASAJI CHIBA, ASIAN INDIGENOUS LAW IN INTERACTION WITH RECEIVED LAW (1986).

10. ALAN WATSON, LEGAL TRANSPLANTS: AN APPROACH TO COMPARATIVE LAW (2d Ed. 1993).

11. These laws are not officially recognised by a state, but exist in social reality. *Compare* CHIBA, *supra* note. 9 (discussing the interaction of official law, unofficial law and "legal postulates") *with* MENSKI, *supra* note.1 (elaborating on the notion)

12. CHIBA, *supra* note 9, at 5-6; MENSKI, *supra* note 1, at 124.

13. Historians and other social scientists often have a far too limited and restrained, positivism-centric understanding of "law" and its possibilities of skilful intervention. *See, e.g.,* SUFIA UDDIN, CONSTRUCTING BANGLADESH: RELIGION,

ETHNICITY AND LANGUAGE IN AN ISLAMIC NATION (2006) (presenting an excellent recent discussion of such academic struggles).

14. John Griffiths, *What is Legal Pluralism?*, 24 JOURNAL OF LEGAL PLURALISM AND UNOFFICIAL LAW 1-56 (1986).

15. Recent studies by Sanskrit-based scholars have brought this out well. Patrick Olivelle has beautifully encapsulated this:

"The expert tradition of Dharma during the centuries immediately preceding the common era appears to have been vibrant and dynamic as shown by the numerous contradictory opinions of experts recorded in the extant Dharmastras. Such diversity of opinion belies the common assumption that ancient Indian society was uniform and stifling under an orthodoxy imposed by Brahmins. If even the experts recorded in these normative texts disagree so vehemently, the reality on the ground must have been even more chaotic and exhilarating".

16. DHAGAMWAR, supra note 3, at 76
(highlighting the danger of widespread public unrest). Some more recent Indian legal writing, inspired from Canada, appears to dismiss such risks and pushes ahead with reformist human rights agenda even if it means suffering for some people. See JAYA SAGADE, CHILD MARRIAGE IN INDIA: SOCIO-LEGAL AND HUMAN RIGHTS DIMENSIONS (2005).

17. India's new Prohibition of Child Marriage Act of 2006 illustrates this interplay. It renders Indian child marriages voidable, not void *ab initio* after judges had warned that it would be "absolutely brutal" to render all child marriages void. WERNER MENSKI, HINDU LAW: BEYOND TRADITION AND MODERNITY 368 (2003) (discussing *V.* Mallikarjunaiah v. H.C. Gowramma, A.I.R. 1997 Kant. 77, at 81).

18. *See Shah Bano*, A.I.R. 1985 S.C. 945.

19. The Muslim Women (Protection of Rights in Divorce) Act, No. 25, Acts of Parliament, 1986.

20. Ali v. Sufaira, (1988) 2 K.L.T. 94; *See also* WERNER MENSKI, MODERN INDIAN FAMILY LAW 246-294 (2001) (discussing a large number of subsequent cases in that High Court and other Indian High Courts).

21. Danial Latifi v. Union of India, (2001) 7 S.C.C. 740.

22. The Muslim Women (Protection of Rights in Divorce) Act, No. 25, Acts of Parliament, 1986.

23. MENSKI, *supra* note 20.

24. Werner Menski, *Introduction: The Democratisation of Justice in India* to GURJEET SINGH, LAW OF CONSUMER PROTECTION IN INDIA: JUSTICE WITHIN REACH xxv-liv (1996).

25. Jaya Sagade, Law and Social Reforms in Rural India with Special Reference to Child Marriages, 1 SUP. CT. J.(1981). See also SAGADE, supra note 16

26. M.P. JAIN, OUTLINES OF INDIAN LEGAL HISTORY (4th ed. 1981); J. DUNCAN M. DERRETT, HINDU LAW PAST AND PRESENT (1957); J. DUNCAN. M. DERRETT, RELIGION, LAW AND THE STATE IN INDIA, Ch.10 (1968).

27. CHIBA, *supra* note 9.

28. WILLIAM TWINING, GLOBALISATION AND LEGAL THEORY (2006).

29. SACK & JONATHAN ALECK, LAW AND ANTHROPOLOGY (1992).

30. *See* Pierre Legrand, *HOW TO COMPARE NOW*, 16 LEGAL STUDIES (No. 2) 232-242, 236 (1996) (discussing the particular mentalité of French law).

31. GEOFFREY A. ODDIE, IMAGINED HINDUISM (2006) (discussing various historical constructions of the image of Hinduism and Hindu law).

32. We should also remember that much of "colonial India" was not under direct British rule, but under what in Africa and elsewhere came to be called "indirect rule", largely retaining local legal and political structures, not to speak of social norms and value systems.

33. M.B. HOOKER, LEGAL PLURALISM (1975).

34. See Raziuddin Aquil, Hazrat-i-Dehli: The Making of the Chishti Sufi Centre and the Stronghold of Islam, 28 SOUTH ASIA RESEARCH (No. 1) 23-48 (2008).

35. MENSKI, *supra* note 17.

36. MENSKI, *supra* note 1, at 294-298.

37. PATRICK GLENN, LEGAL TRADITIONS OF THE WORLD: SUSTAINABLE DIVERSITY IN LAW 51 (2004) (speaking of "a number of globalizations going on").

38. MENSKI, *supra* note 1, at 13.

39. Julius J. Lipner, *The Rise of "Hinduism"; or, How to Invent a World Religion with only Moderate Success*, 10TH INTERNATIONAL JOURNAL OF HINDU STUDIES (No. 1) 91-104 (2006).

40. GLENN, *supra* note 37.

41. While this has had some relevance for legal development in modern India, we cannot explore this further here.

42. Some old reported cases from India, however, show that Muslims sometimes defined Hindus as *kitabiyya* to justify marriage to a Hindu woman. After all, many Hindus also have religious texts and may treat such a text as a kind of holy book, especially the epic Ramayana.

43. JYOTIRMAYA SHARMA, HINDUTVA: EXPLORING THE IDEA OF HINDU NATIONALISM (2003).

44. The predicament of comparability is hardly new: the seven volumes of the *History of Dharmashastra*, originally written towards the end of the colonial period, were partly designed to prove to the colonial

powers that Hindus had "proper" law, even if it meant that Kane often overstated his case. PANDURANG VAMAN KANE, HISTORY OF DHARMASHASTRA (1968) (1930-1962).

45. The storming and destruction of an old mosque in Ayodhya in December 1992 gave rise to huge debates, outrage, as well as communal riots all over India.

46. ANURADHA DINGWANEY NEEDHAM & RAJESWARI SUNDER RAJAN, THE CRISIS OF SECULARISM IN INDIA (2007).

47. INDIAN CONST. Art. 14 (protecting equality before law); INDIAN CONST. Art. 15 (prohibiting discrimination on the grounds of religion, race, caste, sex or place of birth). INDIAN CONST. Arts. 25-28 (concerning the right to freedom of religion); INDIA CONST. Arts. 29-30 (concerning cultural and educational rights).

48. DHAGAMWAR, *supra* note 3, at 76.

49. SAGADE, *supra* note 16.

50. The term "identity postulate" is explained by Chiba as a term focused on construction of identity of a particular people, a set of values and ethics rather than a body of rules. MASAJI CHIBA, LEGAL PLURALISM; TOWARDS A GENERAL THEORY THROUGH JAPANESE LEGAL CULTURE 180 (1989).

51. Notably, my learned predecessor, J.D.M. Derrett, still saw reservations in 1968 about the ability to make law through statutory intervention as an "apparently unpractical point of view". *See* Derrett, *supra* note 26, at 76.

52. MENSKI, *supra* note 17, at 94-107.

53. On Ambedkar's contribution, there is a huge literature. *See* S.K. DHAWAN, DR. B.R. AMBEDKAR: A SELECT PROFILE (1891-1956) (1991); 1 & 2 K.L. CHANCHREEK, DR. B.R. AMBEDKAR: PATRIOT, PHILOSOPHER, STATESMAN: ECONOMIC WRITINGS (1991); NAZEER H. KHAN, B.R. AMBEDKAR ON FEDERALISM, ETHNICITY AND GENDER JUSTICE (2001).

54. Marc Galanter & Jayanth Krishnan, *Personal Law Systems and Religious Conflict, in* RELIGION AND PERSONAL LAW IN SECULAR INDIA: A CALL TO JUDGMENT 270-300 (G.J. Larson ed., 2001) (depicting a typical Anglo-centric statement).

55. GRANVILLE AUSTIN, THE INDIAN CONSTITUTION: CORNERSTONE OF A NATION ix (1999).

56. *See supra* note 53.

57. INDIAN CONST. Art. 44.

58. ANTONY ALLOTT, THE LIMITS OF LAW 216 (1980).

59. Virendra Kumar, *Uniform Civil Code Revisited: A Juridical Analysis of John Vallamattom*, 45 JOURNAL OF THE INDIAN LAW INSTITUTE 315-334 (2003).

60. Werner Menski, *Jaina Law as an Unofficial Legal System, in* PETER FLUEGEL, DISPUTES AND DIALOGUES: STUDIES IN JAINA HISTORY AND CULTURE 417-435 (2006) (discussing the position of Jaina law).

61. In their own way, Pakistan and later Bangladesh did exactly the same for Muslim law, again without complete success in terms of legal unification and reform.

62. Under the Muslim personal law (shari'a), based on Quran'ic verses, up to four wives are allowed to Muslim husbands. In contrast, section 5(i) of the Hindu Marriage Act of 1955 prohibits polygamous marriage for Hindus and makes it a crime under section 17 of the same Act. *See* The Hindu Marriage Act, 1955, No. 25, Acts of Parliament, 1955.

63. MENSKI, *supra* note 20, at 139-230; MENSKI, *supra* note 17, at ch. 10 (attempting to bring the various strands together).

64. *Shah Bano*, A.I.R. 1985 S.C. 945.

65. *Danial Latifi*, (2001) 7 S.C.C. 740.

66. *Supra* note 26.

67. The Hindu Marriage (Amendment) Act, 1964, No. 44, Acts of Parliament, 1964 (adding two new grounds for divorce among Hindus).

68. *See* J. DUNCAN M. DERRETT, A CRITIQUE OF MODERN HINDU LAW (1970).

69. DUNCAN M. DERRETT, THE DEATH OF A MARRIAGE LAW (1978).

70. Bikkar Singh v. Mohinder Kaur, A.I.R. 1981 P&H 391; Balbir Kaur v. Maghar Singh, A.I.R. 1984 P&H 417.

71. MENSKI, *supra* note 20, at 72-138 (examining the relevant case law).

72. RAN HIRSCHL, TOWARDS JURISTOCRACY: THE ORIGINS AND CONSEQUENCES OF THE NEW CONSTITUTIONALISM (2004).

73. *See* Soundarammal v. Sundara Mahalinga Nadar, A.I.R. 1980 Mad. 294.

74. Shah Bano, A.I.R. 1985 S.C. 945. See also Jorden Diengdeh v. S.S. Chopra, A.I.R. 1985 S.C. 935, at 935-936, 940.

75. One of the most recent examples is John Vallamattom v. Union of India, where V. N. Khare, then Chief Justice of India stated that "[i]t is a matter of regret that Art. 44 of the Constitution has not been given effect to. Parliament is still to step in for framing a common civil code in the country. A common civil code will help the cause of national integration by removing the contradictions based on ideologies". Notably, this was two years after the uniformising legal developments analysed in the present article. John Vallamattom v. Union of India, 2003(3) KLT 66 (SC), at 80.

76. Kumar, supra note 59.

77. Sivankutty v. S. Komalakumari, A.I.R. 1989 Ker. 124 (holding that poverty is "a misfortune that has to be shared by the wife also").

78. Gladstone v. Geetha Gladstone, 2002(2) KLT SN 126 (Case No. 155) (holding that "[e]very Indian citizen is bound to maintain his wife and children. That is a tradition of the society").

79. The Hindu Marriage Act, 1955, No. 25, Acts of Parliament, 1955.

80. *See* Kanchan v. Kamalendra, A.I.R. 1992 Bom. 493.

81. In section 125 of the Criminal Procedure Code of 1973, it is provided under Explanation (b) that "'wife' includes a woman who has been divorced by, or has obtained a divorce from, her husband and has not remarried".

82. Shah Bano, A.I.R. 1985 S.C. 945.

83. Bai Tahira v. Ali Hussain Chothia, A.I.R. 1979 S.C. 362 and (1979) 2 S.C.C. 316.

84. Shah Bano, A.I.R. 1985 S.C. 945, at 952 (holding that there is "no doubt that the Quran imposes an obligation on the Muslim husband to make provision for or to provide maintenance to the divorced wife. The contrary argument does less then justice to the teachings of the Quran").

85. Ashutosh Varshney, *The Great Indian Political Churning*, INDIA TODAY INTERNATIONAL, July 2, 2007, at 12-13 (claiming that "caught in a Muslim furore and understanding it little, Rajiv Gandhi used his three-fourth majority in the Lok Sabha to overturn the court's judgment"). This is serious misrepresentation of legal facts by a political scientist, even in 2007, and one really has to wonder who understands little, the Indian politician with his ear to the ground, or the NRI academic.

86. S.P. SATHE, JUDIAL ACTIVISM IN INDIA: TRANSGRESSING BORDERS AND ENFORCING LIMITS 19 (2002).

87. The Muslim Women (Protection of Rights on Divorce) Act, 1986, No. 25, Acts of Parliament, 1986.

88. Varshney, *supra* note 85; SATHE, *supra* note 86.

89. Secretary, Tamil Nadu Waqf Board v. Syed Fatima Nachi, A.I.R. 1996 S.C. 2423; Noor Saba Khatoon v. Mohd. Quasim (1997) 6 S.C.C. 233.

90. Ali v. Sufaira, (1988) 2 K.L.T. 94; *See also* MENSKI, *supra* note 20, at 231-94 (discussing a large number of subsequent cases in that High Court and other Indian High Courts).

91. Sylvia Vatuk, *Where Will She Go? What Will She Do? Paternalism Toward Women in the Administration of Muslim Personal Law in Contemporary India*, *in* RELIGION AND PERSONAL LAW IN SECULAR INDIA: A CALL TO JUDGMENT 226-248 (G.J. Larson ed., 2001*)*; Galanter, *supra* note 54.

92. Werner Menski, Double Benefits and Muslim Women's Postnuptial Rights, KERALA LAW TIMES, 2007(2), at 21-34.

93. Ahammed v. Aysha, 1990 (1) KLT 172.

94. Danial Latifi, (2001) 7 S.C.C. 740.

95. In 1976, the Marriage Laws (Amendment) Act inserted section 13(2)(iv) into the original Hindu Marriage Act, permitting a Hindu wife exit through divorce from a marriage into which she had been virtually forced, a rule taken from Muslim law. *See* the Marriage Laws (Amendment) Act, 1976, No. 68, Acts of Parliament, 1976.

96. Flavia Agnes, *Interview with Tanu Thomas K.*, THE TIMES OF INDIA, Aug.29, 2003 (stressing that "the press has chosen to ignore it and the general public is unaware of it").

97. Menski, *supra* note 92.

98. Werner Menski, *Reluctant Legislative Activism*, KERALA LAW TIMES, 2004(1), at 35-41.

99. Vatuk, *supra* note 91.

100. The Maintenance and Welfare of Parents and Senior Citizens Act of 2007.

101. Tahir Mahmood, Personal Laws in Crisis (1986) (discussing the early warnings).

102. But Indian Muslim women can, and apparently do, use the quite liberal provisions of the Dissolution of Muslim Marriages Act, 1939.

103. Mary Sonia Zachariah v. Union of India, 1995(1) KLT 644 (FB).

104. The Indian Divorce (Amendment) Act, 2001, No. 51, Acts of Parliament, 2001, § 10(2).

105. MENSKI, *supra* note 7.

*****

www.ingramcontent.com/pod-product-compliance
Lightning Source LLC
Chambersburg PA
CBHW050116230526
45470CB00004B/1855